Persian Textile Designs

Mehry Motamen Reid

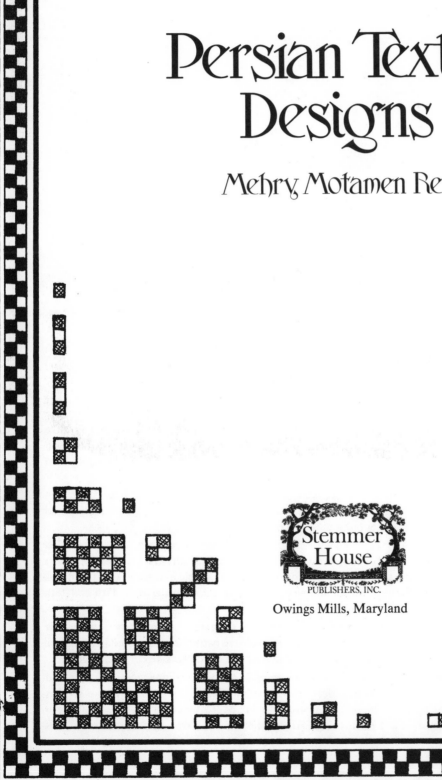

Stemmer
House
PUBLISHERS, INC.

Owings Mills, Maryland

INTRODUCTION

No one knows exactly how or when our ancestors began to weave fibers into textiles. Some say men and women first learned how to weave grass into mats and baskets. This process may have suggested to them that they could do the same with wool from sheep. Certainly in early times animal skins were used for clothing. But eventually, tribespeople found that a garment woven from wool was more comfortable to wear than the skin of sheep or other animals.

Various people discovered weaving independently in different parts of the world. The people of Mesopotamia, including the Persians, may have learned the weaving art as early as the Egyptians. Persia (Iran), a country located in southwestern Asia, is a rugged land of snow-capped mountains, green valleys and barren deserts, and is one of the oldest countries in the world. Its history goes back over 5,000 years.

In about 2700 B.C., a princess of China developed silk weaving, while Persia, on the silk-trade route from China, also produced fine fabrics. They are known to us by means of preserved specimens (often found in church treasuries) and from representations in rock reliefs. Heraldically stylized animals, of which the fantastic peacock dragon is the best known, prevailed.

The Persian silks exercised great influence on other materials (metal, ceramics, stucco tiles). They were also appreciated outside the country in Byzantium and Egypt. Even the Far East imitated them or used them as a source of inspiration. Chinese influence is strongly felt in decorative Persian arts as well, especially through the introduction of Chinese motifs such as the lotus, the dragon, the phoenix, and cloud symbols. Fabric and carpet-weaving evolved from small workshop industries to become major manifestations of Persian art.

The designs of wool and silk tapestries may be centralized, or else organized into an all-over pattern. We can find trees, flowers, real and fantastic animals, men and women, fruits and gardens or woods, both earthly and heavenly in Persian textile designs, as well as the popular paisley patterns.

In addition to pure silk textiles, silk was often woven with metal threads. Metal threads are, in fact, the oldest form of man-made fiber, dating back to the period of early Persia and Assyria. Actually, the first metallic fibers were not true fibers but very thin sheets of metal in narrow ribbonlike forms. Usually real gold and silver were the metals used in old Persian textiles, as well as in floral brocades and silk taffetas and satins in the 16th, 17th and 18th centuries.

Persians were highly skilled weavers of wool, silk, linen, cotton and flax. Originally, all fabrics were plain. The first designs were probably painted, then later embroidered. Many embroidery patterns are depicted in miniature paintings. After the Moslem religion (Islam) was carried by Arabs all over Persia, designs began to change.

The story behind this change is an interesting one. Before Mohammed, Arabs worshipped idols. Mohammed himself believed in Allah, the "one true God." He set out to destroy the worship of idols. But he found that as soon as he turned his back, his followers would make new idols. To put an end to this, Mohammed forbade the Moslems to draw, carve, paint or embroider likenesses of any living things. Artists and weavers soon began to get around this edict by changing animal forms so that they were no longer true to life. They would draw a bird's head on backwards, or divide a form into little sections. This is called "conventionalized" design; that is, the forms have been changed into pure decoration and are no longer "naturalistic."

At this time and later, an animal or bird form in a circle, called a roundel, was a favorite textile design in Persia.

In addition, the country folk of Persia like to make bright floral designs using strong shades of primary colors. If one looks at a gathering of women on a festive occasion, it is like seeing a garden of bright spring flowers clustered together. The fabrics they favor are usually in floral patterns; however, plain colors may also be mixed in interesting and beautiful combinations in the same garment, and decorated with varicolored ribbons. The material is usually silk taffeta, satin, chiffon, harir (very fine chiffon), or toor (lace). Fine cotton fabrics (cheet, chelvar, metghal, dabit) are also used as well as velvet — a silk-cotton mixture, and brocade — a mixture of silk and metallic threads. Country menfolk wear a type of cotton shirt with a white background and either a fine black stripe or else checked patterns of red, blue or black with white.

Some cotton and silk patterns are not woven into the material but rather are stamped on. One can tell the use to which a fabric is to be put by the pattern. For example, some patterns are used only for tablecloths, bedspreads or the covering cloths of bundles, and these are usually fringed with metal thread.

The textiles of Persia reflect the love of her people for beauty in color and design, a small sampling of which is presented in this book.

M.M.R.

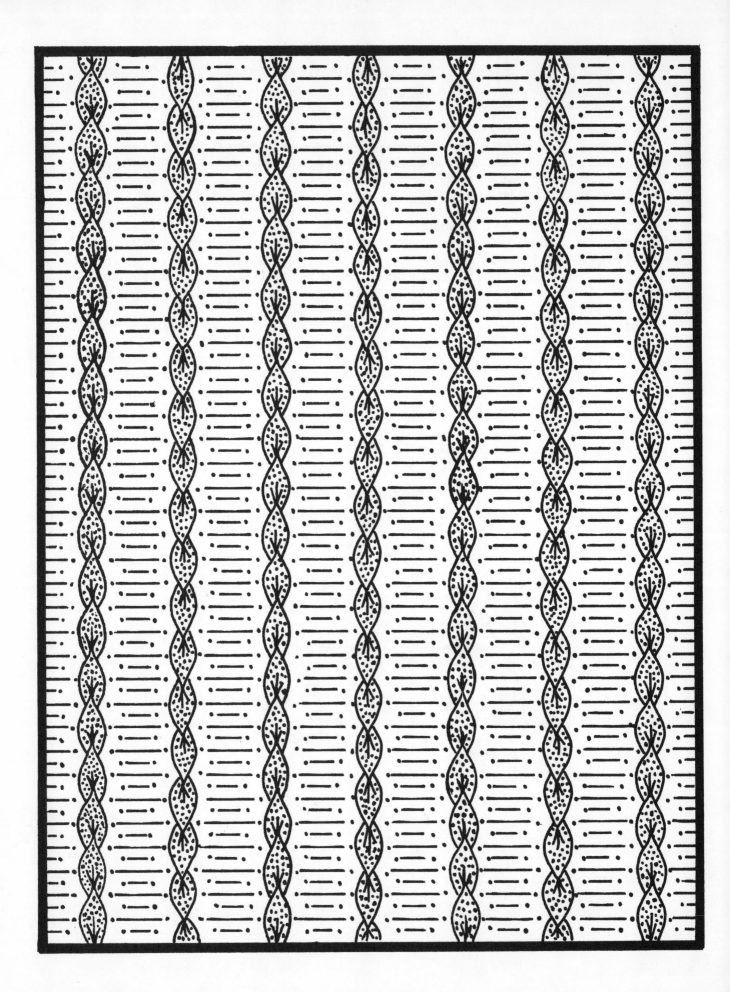

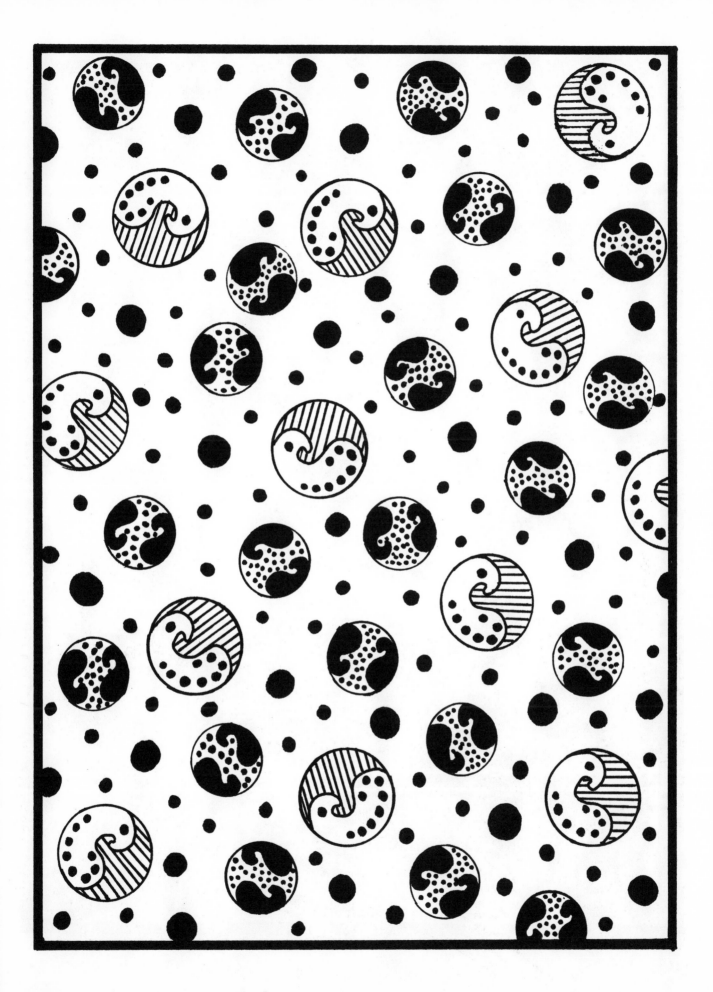

Designed by Barbara Holdridge
Composed by Typographic Service, Inc.
    Philadelphia, Pennsylvania
Cover printed by Strine Printing Co., Inc.
    York, Pennsylvania
Printed and bound by Port City Press, Inc.
    Baltimore, Maryland, on 75-pound Williamsburg Offset